DUNROBIN CASTLE

Jewel in the Crown of the Highlands

CONTENTS

TOUR
OF THE
CASTLE

Main Entrance

You enter the Castle through the main front door just as the Duke would have done after debarking from his yacht in 1850 and coming up a steep hill from the shore in a coach and four. As you enter, to your right is another set of steps up which the luggage is taken to the luggage room. Once inside the hall the first thing you see is a huge coat-of-arms above the fireplace; this relates to the 2nd Duke of Sutherland (1786-1861) who more than tripled the size of the Castle in the period 1845-1850. A wide shallow set of steps in front of you takes you up to an upper level where you can turn left through the garden door to look out at the Gardens, Museum and the very exciting Falconry display, or you can turn right into the main body of the Castle.

FRANGAS·NON·FLECTES

SANS

PEUR

Cornice

1. Duke of Sutherland
2. Married Arms of 8th Duke of Argyll who married, 1844, Elizabeth, eldest daughter of the 2nd Duke of Sutherland
3. Married Arms of the 12th Lord Blantyre who married, 1843, Evelyn, second daughter of the 2nd Duke of Sutherland
4. Married Arms of the 4th Duke of Leinster, who, as Marquess of Kildare married, 1847, Caroline, third daughter of the 2nd Duke of Sutherland
5. Married Arms of George Granville William, Marquess of Stafford, later 3rd Duke of Sutherland, who married, 1849, Anne, in her own right Countess of Cromartie
6. Married Arms of the 2nd Duke of Sutherland (left half of shield his own Arms, right half Howard).

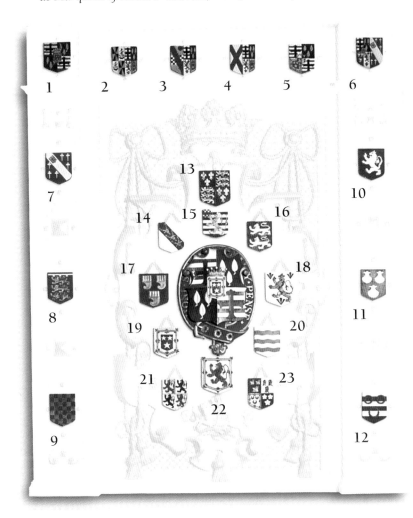

Centre Panel

Arms of Leveson-Gower, Duke of Sutherland (centre) surrounded by principal Arms quartered by 2nd Duke in right of descent from heiresses.

Through his father:
13. King Henry VII
14. Barony of Stanley
15. Clifford, Earl of Cumberland, on a Canton Brandon Duke of Suffolk
16. Barony of Strange of Knockin
17. Granville, Earl of Bath and through his mother, Elizabeth, in her own right, Countess of Sutherland
18. Egerton, Duke of Bridgewater and through his mother:

19. Sutherland
20. Drummond, Earl of Perth
21. Wemyss, Earl of Wemyss
22. King Robert the Bruce
23. Gordon

Palister

Arms of Lady Harriet Howard:
7. Howard
   Principal quarterings
8. Brotherton
9. Mowbray
10. Surrey
11. Dacre
12. Greystock

THE ARMORIAL PANEL

This panel illustrates the armorial achievement of George Granville, 2nd Duke of Sutherland; his wife, Lady Harriet Howard, daughter of the 6th Earl of Carlisle; and their children.

THE MAIN STAIRCASE

The main staircase epitomises the impression that the Duke and Duchess wanted to create, that of an enormous palace dedicated to the entertainment of their friends and relations. It contains a collection of hunting trophies (and indeed a whole red stag) which indicates the Castle's use as one of the largest hunting lodges in Scotland. Throughout the Castle there are wonderful arrangements of flowers.

Top: Duchess Eileen, wife of the 5th Duke of Sutherland

Middle: 1st Duke of Sutherland by W. Owen RA

Right: Duchess Millicent, wife of the 4th Duke of Sutherland by Ellis Roberts

A bronze bust of Duchess Eileen

THE GALLERY

At the top of the main stairs, turn left into the Gallery where you will see a large billiard table and one striking picture; *The 3rd Duke and his sister Lady Evelyn*, by Sir Edwin Landseer and also an unique instrument; an Aeolian Orchestrelle built in Connecticut, USA in 1904. This amazing invention is an automatic organ and uses a roll of punched paper to control the notes it plays. On your way back to the top of the stairs you will notice two very fine Boulle cabinets containing trophies, from the time when the Castle was temporarily used as a school from 1965 to 1972.

The 3rd Duke and his sister Lady Evelyn by Sir Edwin Landseer

THE DINING ROOM

This is the first of the major Victorian public rooms and is laid for dinner in exactly the same way as it would have been in 1850. It contains a wonderful collection of family portraits, the best of which is on the left depicting *William, 18th Earl of Sutherland* by Allan Ramsay (No. 226). Going clockwise round the room there are the *Children of the 1st Duke of Sutherland,* by Thomas Phillips, above the fireplace (No. 220). The children are Lady Sophia (later Duchess of Norfolk), Lady Elizabeth (later Marchioness of Westminster) and Lord Francis Egerton (later Earl of Ellesmere). Next is *Granville, 1st Marquess of Stafford* by George Romney. Lord Stafford held important court and governmental posts including Master of the Horse, Lord Chamberlain and Lord Privy Seal. He was the father of the 1st Duke of Sutherland. At the end of the room hangs *Harriet Duchess of Sutherland* by Sir Thomas Lawrence (No. 155). She was the daughter of the 6th Earl of Carlisle and wife of the 2nd Duke of Sutherland and became Mistress of the Robes to Queen Victoria. On her knee is her eldest daughter Elizabeth, afterwards Duchess of Argyll. Between the windows are portraits of *1st Duke of Sutherland* and of *Lady Caroline Leveson-Gower,* afterwards Countess of Carlisle, both painted by Romney.

Duchess Harriet with her eldest daughter Elizabeth on her knee by Sir Thomas Lawrence

Lady Caroline Leveson-Gower, sister of the 1st Duke of Sutherland by George Romney, 1778

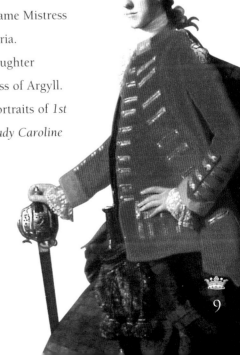

18th Earl of Sutherland by Alan Ramsay

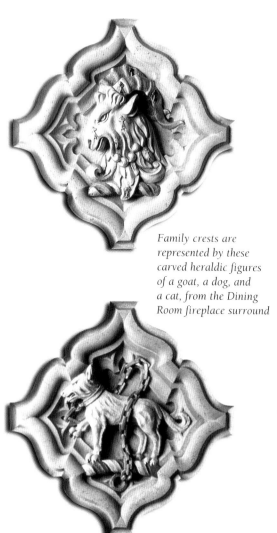

Family crests are
represented by these
carved heraldic figures
of a goat, a dog, and
a cat, from the Dining
Room fireplace surround

Duchess Harriet, wife of the 2nd Duke of Sutherland, by Winterhalter

The final portrait in the room is of *Harriet, Duchess of Sutherland,* by Winterhalter. It is felt nowadays that she was mainly responsible for the enlargement of Dunrobin, the recreation of Trentham Hall, the rebuilding of Cliveden, and the building of what is now Lancaster House next to Buckingham Palace.

The room features a Khorassan carpet. The oak chairs of the Stuart period design are covered in needlework by Duchess Eileen, wife of the 5th Duke.

A detail of the Italian frieze

THE MUSIC ROOM

Hugh O'Neil, 2nd Earl of Tyrone, by Michael Wright

There are several pictures in the Music Room, the first of which is the portrait by Michael Wright of an *Irish Chieftain, said to be Hugh O'Neil, 2nd Earl of Tyrone (1540-1616) in native Irish dress, with a suit of Japanese armour in the foreground.* Above the fireplace hangs the portrait of a *Venetian Procurator* by Tintoretto. Then going around the room, *Lady Helen Sutherland* by Henry Smith, *Alexander 12th Earl of Sutherland* by an unknown artist and *Lady Janet Sutherland* by Henry Smith, *Mrs Barry* by Kneller and *The Young Female Artist* by George Watson

This room is frequently used for small concerts.

THE BREAKFAST ROOM

The Victorians were very keen on having separate rooms for separate functions, hence a special room for having breakfast. Only the gentlemen had breakfast in this room, while the ladies were served breakfast in their rooms upstairs. On the left of the door by which you enter, there is a wonderful portrait by Hoppner of the *Duchess-Countess* and below it a superb picture of the *The Breakfast* by Sir David Wilkie (1785-1841).

Between the windows is a family portrait of *William, Earl of Sutherland and Elizabeth Wemyss, Countess of Sutherland, their children; William, Lord Strathnaver, afterwards 18th Earl of Sutherland* (father of the Duchess-Countess) *and Lady Elizabeth*, who was to marry her cousin, James Wemyss. It was the 11th Earl of Wemyss who took a keen interest in Weymss-ware pottery, a collection of which can be seen in the Queen's Corridor. There is another fine Michael Wright of *John Granville, Earl of Bath (1628-1701)*; Granville is a name much associated with the Sutherland family.

Marble bust of the 1st Duke of Sutherland

Elizabeth Duchess-Countess by Sir Thomas Lawrence

Above the fireplace there is a portrait of *Serena* by George Romney, above the serving table is another portrait of the *Duchess-Countess* by Sir Thomas Lawrence, and to her left are two superb Ramsays, one of *Lady Margaret Weymss, Countess of Moray* and the lower and better one of *Mary Maxwell*, the wife of the 18th Earl in the red coat in the Dining Room. The portrait of Mary Maxwell is one of the best that Ramsay ever did when he was at the height of his prowess. Finally, there is a good portrait on panel of *Sir Alexander Gordon of Navidale* dated 1631; Navidale is just north of Helmsdale and the Gordons were a powerful local family in the 16th and 17th centuries.

Mary Maxwell, wife of the 18th Earl of Sutherland by Allan Ramsay

The Breakfast
by Sir David Wilkie

The chair in the picture is still in the possession of Lord Crawford in Fife and his father offered the present Countess the possibility of swapping the chair for the picture; she declined. The old lady sitting at the table is thought to be Wilkie's mother.

15

THE DRAWING ROOM

This magnificent room was designed by Sir Robert Lorimer after the fire, which took place in this end of the Castle in 1915. The fire very nearly destroyed the building altogether, and it was only put out by the lucky arrival of hundreds of sailors from Royal Navy ships which were lying off the coast. At that time, the Castle was a Naval Hospital and they were therefore very keen to make sure that nothing untoward happened to their shipmates. Apparently, they ran along the top of the roof carrying a bucket of water in each hand, forming human chains and thus extinguishing a major blaze. Lorimer decided that the Castle needed a spacious French salon and so combined two rooms to create a light and spacious room, in direct contrast to the cosy clutter of the Victorian era and giving fine views of the gardens and parterres surrounding the large fountains.

The principal items of furniture are of the Louis XV period and comprise a set to two settees and twelve fauteuils ensuite with draught screens, but the star is the Louis XVI French table with the Florentine pietra dura top made by Joseph Baumhauer between 1745 and 1772.

This room is also available for weddings and functions.

17

The *Canalettos* over the fireplace are actually by Fyador (Yakavlegich) Alekseyev and show two different views of the Doge's Palace in Venice painted in the late 1770s in the style of Canaletto. They are not copies; they are pastiches. The walls are hung with 18th century Mortlake tapestries depicting scenes from the life of Diogenes (412-325 B.C.), the Greek Cynic philosopher. Among the incidents depicted are *Diogenes and Dionysus, Diogenes being visited by Alexander the Great* and *Diogenes contemplating death.*

Detail of the fine carving on the Drawing Room fireplace

The portraits between the windows starting by the piano, are of the *2nd Duke of Sutherland* by Sir Thomas Lawrence and below him is his sister *Elizabeth, later Countess Belgrave* also by Sir Thomas Lawrence. In the next bay the upper portrait is of *John, 14th Earl of Sutherland* painted at the age of 60 in 1660; He died at the age of 71 having established the Sutherland Clan as the leading military force in the north-east of Scotland. He served his apprenticeship on the Continent where he learnt all the latest military tricks of the trade and came home to put them

Two portraits of Elizabeth, Duchess-Countess of Sutherland; by John Hoppner (above), and below, by the leading portrait painter of the day, Sir Joshua Reynolds

to good effect. Below him is another portrait of the *2nd Duke of Sutherland* as a young man by Phillips. In the next bay the upper portrait is of *Frederick the 5th Elector of Palatine* by Mirevelt. He is the direct ancestor of HM Queen Elizabeth II. The lower portrait is another one of the *Duchess-Countess,* this one by Sir Joshua Reynolds (1728-1792), the leading portrait painter of his day. In the 4th bay the upper portrait is again of the *Duchess-Countess* this time by John Hoppner and the lower portrait is a magnificent Lawrence of *Lord Francis Leveson-Gower later Lord Francis Egerton 1st Earl of Ellesmere*; he is the direct ancestor of the present Duke of Sutherland. (See family tree on page 48) This room is also used for concerts and has the most wonderful acoustics, partly because of Lorimer's tremendous ceiling. One of his attributes was the ability to get excellent work from experienced artisans, and this ceiling recreates the armorial achievement of the 2nd Duke of Sutherland (as in the Entrance Hall).

THE LIBRARY

Sir Robert Lorimer formed this room from a
principal bedroom and a dressing room. It is lined
throughout with sycamore wood.

The focal point of this room is the portrait by
Philip de Laszlo of *Duchess Eileen*. Born Lady
Eileen Butler, elder daughter of the Earl or
Lanesborough, she married the 5th Duke of
Sutherland in 1912. The Duchess, who was
Mistress of the Robes to Queen Mary, died in 1943.

19

On the opposite wall hangs a portrait of the 5th Duke painted in 1901 when he was Marquess of Stafford. This portrait was a gift from the tenantry of Dunrobin Estate to mark Lord Stafford's coming-of-age.

The Library houses over 10,000 books, many of them fine and rare editions. The furniture includes a Chippendale mahogany pedestal library table, Georgian reading rest, 19th century globe by the Edinburgh firm W. & A.K. Johnstone, a long case clock by J. Hanley and a Regency mahogany circular rent table. Many of the books in the Library relate to Scots Law and also to the development of the Scottish Highlands in the 19th century.

When you visit the Museum in the Gardens please remember the two portraits in the Library as these are the two people who furnished the contents of the front room in the Museum.

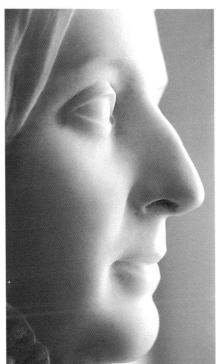

Leaving the Library you come into the Queen's Corridor which is lined with family portraits and also contains a bust of *Harriet, wife of the 2nd Duke of Sutherland* whose portrait by Winterhalter you saw in the Dining Room. Above her is a watercolour by Eugene Lami, painted in 1849, showing a huge reception in the central hall of Stafford House (now Lancaster House). You can just see Queen Victoria in the middle of the grand staircase. These receptions were very fashionable and were known as Crushes; you put on your finest clothes and stood and talked for two or three hours with neither food nor drink. The Queen's Corridor leads you to the charming Ladies' Sitting Room.

The Ladies' Sitting Room

The tapestries on the walls were commissioned for Queen Victoria's visit in 1872, and a picture of Dunrobin is woven into the centre of two of them.

Traditionally this room was used as a quiet place for the ladies of the house to pursue such hobbies as embroidery, gros point, and petit point tapestry, and the free exchange of information.

Leaving the Ladies' Sitting Room you come to a circular staircase to enter the 18th century part of the Castle. Please be very careful on the staircase; its intricate design makes it easy to slip. Access to the upper floors is by way of an oak panelled tower staircase to the Green and Gold Room.

THE GREEN AND
GOLD ROOM

The actual room where Queen Victoria slept is now part of the Library and her sitting room part of the Drawing Room, Lorimer having put together four small rooms to create the present Drawing Room and Library. The Green and Gold Room and adjoining Dressing Room were redecorated in the French style for Duchess Eileen in 1921, the original room having been made in 1785 when the Countess of Sutherland married Lord Stafford. A Gobelin tapestry hangs on the wall opposite the windows and the curtains have a leaf design – an heraldic allusion to the Leveson family. Over the fireplace is a portrait of *The daughter of the Duc de Bourbon* by Nattier. At the head of the bed is a pastel of *Louise, Queen of Prussia* by Madame Vigée le Brun.

Mlle de Sens, daughter of the Duc de Bourbon by Nattier

Lousia, Queen of Prussia by Madame Vigée le Brun

The remainder of the suite consists of a Dressing Room and Bathroom. This was the first bathroom installed in the Castle, in a stone room, which was built on the top of the flat roof of the corridor below. Before this bathroom was constructed, the Duchess took her bath in front of the fire in her dressing room. In the 18th century the bathwater was simply poured out of the window after she had finished but once Victorians built the terrace in 1850, this practice ceased and the water had to be taken away by hand.

The Green and Gold Dressing Room reflected in the mirrored wardrobe doors

Passing another portrait of the *5th Duke of Sutherland in Naval uniform*, also by De Lazlo, you come to the 17th century section of the Castle and The Nursery.

One of four individual doves, decorating the bed, made especially for Queen Victoria's visit in 1872

THE NURSERY

In the Day Nursery, which is lined with sycamore wood, the children of the family and its visitors amused themselves under the supervision of their nannies and nursery maids, not to mention a governess or two. This charming room is also known as the Cromartie Room as Lord Cromartie was arrested here in 1746 having briefly taken the Castle from the Earl of Sutherland; Lord Cromartie was a Jacobite and supported Bonnie Prince Charlie and Cromartie's son, brother and nephew were all executed for their role in the 1745 Rebellion.

He was spared because of a petition presented to the King by his wife and was banished to Devon. The toys on display include a rocking horse and a doll's house, which was made for the present Countess of Sutherland's daughter, Lady Annabel. The model of a 'Zulu' class fishing boat was made sometime before 1921 by local fisherman Donald "Davie" Sutherland. The original boat was named "*Duchess Millicent*" but when Mr Sutherland lost the annual fishing boat race for the first time, he renamed the model "*Marchioness of Golspie*".

In the cabinet is displayed a charming Minton dinner service decorated with kittens at play.

THE NIGHT NURSERY

The Night Nursery has beds for two children. All the furniture is painted, wooden and Sicilian, and was brought to the Castle at the end of the 19th century by the 4th Duke who had spent the winter in Sicily in a rented monastery recovering from a bout of bronchitis. This room demonstrates that you get a better class of souvenir if you have a very large yacht. The bathroom is extremely ingenious; after the Duchess's bathroom was built, a method of having a lot of bathrooms was needed and they hit upon the idea of removing all the circular staircases and replacing them with round bathrooms with specially designed baths and very powerful taps and waste pipes.

THE NANNY'S ROOM is the next room.

Please note the small child's bath in front of the fire and the hot water container that looks like a watering can that would have been used to fill it. The nanny slept in this room with a smaller child in a cot and a baby.

THE DUKE'S STUDY

This room is panelled in Scottish larch. You have now returned to the 18th century part of the Castle.

The portraits on the wall facing the fireplace are of *Alexander, 12th Earl of Sutherland, Lady Jean Gordon, Countess of Sutherland Sir Robert Gordon* and between the windows *William, 17th Earl of Sutherland (1708-1750)* by Henry Smith.

Lady Jean Gordon,
Countess of Sutherland

32

Mary Queen of Scots

After the fire in 1915, the Scottish architect, Sir Robert Lorimer, altered the top of the main tower and clock tower at the north side of the building to the Scottish Renaissance style.

In 1850, having finished the final wing of the Castle, architect Sir Charles Barry turned his attention to the Garden. He designed a smaller version of the vast Italianate garden he had recently completed for the 2nd Duke's Staffordshire Estate at Trentham. At its height the head gardener's domain comprised: two walled gardens including fruit and vegetables and flower borders inside and out; back-up nursery gardens and greenhouses; and beyond, extensive parkland with walks and coastal views. Although much of this has now reverted to woodland, the surviving East Walled Garden with its three parterres each surrounding a pool and fountain provides a perfect layout to view from the Castle and terrace and a fitting foreground to the panoramic view across the Moray Firth to the distant Cairngorm Mountains. Make your way down and you will find a jewel of a garden, full of colour, interest and unexpected features, nestling amongst sheltering trees on a raised shingle beach; from here the Castle towering above provides a splendid backdrop.

Dunrobin is not a garden that only looks back. A small, dedicated team combines a continuity of generations-old gardening skills with careful use of up-to-date horticultural techniques to maintain, develop and take forward what remains.

The Gulf Stream of warm sea-water which flows from the Gulf of Mexico across the Atlantic and brings sub-tropical conditions to western gardens from the Isles of Scilly to the North-west Highlands goes on to sweep round Cape Wrath and John O'Groats making its final influence felt here at Dunrobin on the North coast of the Moray Firth. Several clumps of giant rhubarb *Gunnera manicata* attract comment as their leaves unfurl to their full size of up to 8ft across. A native of S. Brazil and Columbia, it thrives in the mild winters and shelters between the castle and the sea. Fuchsias too thrive at Dunrobin, previous head gardeners raised their own varieties and *Fuchsia 'Dunrobin Bedder'* may still be seen in the borders as well as bold clumps of *Fuchsia magellanica var. molinae* with its flowers of palest shell pink and great banks of *Fuchsia magellanica 'Riccartonii'* with masses of small crimson and purple flowers.

Three box-edged parterres of ascending antiquity carry a succession of colourful floral displays round the garden as the season progresses. April sees early tulips in the lily fountain beds and week by week spring bedding then summer bedding schemes interspersed with displays of perennial geraniums and lilies take the season through to finish with a blaze of late-summer dahlias. Backed by the retaining wall of the Castle Terrace the Duchess Border, dating in its present form from the 1920s, is a majestic sight. Long summer days so far north make for exceptionally tall herbaceous plants and between the buttresses of the wall, Californian lilacs flower with early 20th century climbing hybrid tea roses, now rarely seen.

Also enjoying the warm influence is *Choisya ternata* the Mexican orange blossom forming clipped evergreen mounds in a sheltered corner, its heavily-scented white flowers attracting butterflies and moths on summer evenings.

A fine line of clipped topiary whitebeams and a maturing line of red hawthorns in wooden tubs are recent developments which echo the garden's Italianate origins. Nearby a new garden in the style of a 19th century French potager and featuring 20 giant wooden pyramid plant supports is the boldest project to date and frames a new vista across the garden.

The carved detail on one of the Pictish stones

The figure-head from the 3rd Duke's yatch 'Catania'

THE MUSEUM

Built in 1732 by William, Earl of Sutherland, as a Summer House and extended in 1878 by the 3rd Duke, the Museum houses a collection of hunting trophies and other items brought from all over the world, together with many objects of interest presented to the Museum by friends of the Sutherland family.

The Pictish stones form a very important collection, giving an opportunity to study the devices carved on stones 1,500 years ago. There is also a section on geology, gold panning at Kildonan, and the coal mine at Brora.

The 3rd Duke of Sutherland as a boy by Zoi de Fabeck

School in Golspie and fought industrial diseases in the Potteries. Duchess Millicent was a great late Victorian and Edwardian hostess and the Sutherlands' London residence, Stafford House, was the scene of many brilliant parties and literary receptions. Stafford House was then the largest and most splendid of all London houses, outstripping even Devonshire House and Londonderry House. Always Crown property, it survives to this day, just off the Mall, as Lancaster House, a Government hospitality centre.

Cromartie, 4th Duke, was like the three previous Dukes, a Knight of the Garter and Lord Lieutenant of Sutherland. His wife, the tall and beautiful Duchess Millicent, was a daughter of the 4th Earl of Rosslyn. She was a more successful philanthropist than the 1st Duke, doing endless good works amongst the people on her husband's English and Scottish estates. She was nicknamed 'Meddlesome Millie' and is immortalised as 'The Countess of Chell' in Arnold Bennett's *The Card*. She invented the Highland Home Industries, arranged the trademark for Harris Tweed, built a Technical

The Duchess's elder son, the 5th Duke of Sutherland, held several ministerial offices, having served both in the Army and the Royal Navy in the Great War. His first wife was Lady Eileen Butler, elder daughter of the 7th Earl of Lanesborough.

Her portrait by de Laszlo is the most striking feature of the Library. His second wife, Clare, Duchess of Sutherland, survived him. When the 5th Duke died in

Lord Alistair, father of the present Countess

1963 without issue he was succeeded in all his estates by his niece Elizabeth, only daughter of his younger brother Lord Alistair Sutherland-Leveson-Gower M.C. who had died in 1921.

Miss Elizabeth Sutherland-Leveson-Gower became Countess of Sutherland in her own right and the 24th holder of the title. She is also the third woman and the third Elizabeth to inherit the earldom. She was married to Mr. Charles Janson, who died recently, and they have three sons and a daughter. Her eldest son, Lord Strathnaver, is the heir. The dukedom of Sutherland, a United Kingdom title which could not pass through heirs female, was inherited by the 5th Duke's nearest male relative. This was John Egerton, 5th Earl of Ellesmere, a descendant of the second son of the 1st Duke. There was thus in 1963 a complete break between the dukedom and the Sutherland and Staffordshire estates.

To understand the succession and the change in name we have to go back to the 1st Marquess of Stafford, father of the 1st Duke of Sutherland. Lord Stafford married Lady Louisa Egerton, a great heiress. She was the daughter of the 1st

Duke of Bridgwater and under the terms of the will of his 4th son, the 3rd and last Duke of Bridgwater, all his magnificent art collection and immense wealth went to his nephew Lady Louisa Egerton's son, George Granville Leveson-Gower, 1st Duke of Sutherland and thereafter to the latter's second son.

On the death, therefore, of the 1st Duke of Sutherland, the Bridgwater inheritance passed to his second son, Lord Francis Leveson-Gower, who changed his name to Egerton and was created Earl of Ellesmere and Viscount Brackley. These titles merged with the Dukedom of Sutherland, the Marquessate of Stafford, the Earldom of Gower and the Gower baronetcy in the person of the late 6th Duke and now rest with the 7th Duke of Sutherland who lives at Mertoun, St. Boswell's on Tweedside.

For the 6th Duke, the succession meant little more than a change of title, but the ancient Earldom of Sutherland was then, after nearly 140 years, a separate title once more and unlikely ever to be merged with the dukedom again. In Sutherland, then, Dunrobin Castle, the largest house in the Scottish Highlands, remains as a monument to the five Dukes who, for nearly two centuries, were compelled by their status, possessions and connections to undertake the difficult task of living as both English grandees and Highland lairds.

FALCONRY

There could be no more fitting backdrop to an airborne golden eagle, than the towering facade of Dunrobin Castle. Throughout the season, visitors can enjoy displays of the ancient art of falconry by a consumate expert in the field, our resident Falconer, Andy Hughes.

Flying demonstrations of these magnificent birds are conducted on the lawn in the Gardens and feature spectacular birds of prey such as the golden eagle and peregrine falcon, both resident birds in the Scottish Highlands. Additional attractions include more exotic species such as the beautiful South American Chilean Blue eagle, and owls such as the splendid European eagle owl and the beautiful and ethereal barn owl.

Falconry was originally developed many centuries ago as a means of hunting fast or difficult prey as food for the table, and is still practised for this purpose in many parts of the world today. In the Middle East, our peregrine's cousins, the saker and lanner falcons are used, while in the Siberian steppes of Russia, golden eagles are used to hunt and bring down wolves and other large mammals.

Falconer Andy Hughes with his eagle owl

A pair of peregrine falcons

Barn owl

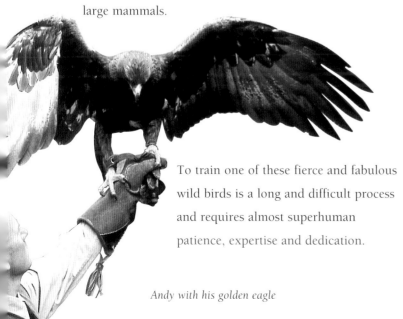

To train one of these fierce and fabulous wild birds is a long and difficult process and requires almost superhuman patience, expertise and dedication.

Andy with his golden eagle

PLAN OF THE CASTLE AND GROUNDS

N

Car and Coach park

Castle Bank

Lower Terrace

Fuchsia Beds

Main Parterre

Grove of Tall Trees

Croquet Lawn

Elm Trees

Falconry Display

Westminster Gate

Watercolour by Nick McCann